QUESTIONS EXPLORED

WHAT IS FAKE NEWS?

by A. R. Carser

BrightPoint Press

San Diego, CA

© 2023 BrightPoint Press
an imprint of ReferencePoint Press, Inc.
Printed in the United States

For more information, contact:
BrightPoint Press
PO Box 27779
San Diego, CA 92198
www.BrightPointPress.com

ALL RIGHTS RESERVED.

No part of this work covered by the copyright hereon may be reproduced or used in any form or by any means—graphic, electronic, or mechanical, including photocopying, recording, taping, web distribution, or information storage retrieval systems—without the written permission of the publisher.

LIBRARY OF CONGRESS CATALOGING-IN-PUBLICATION DATA

Names: Carser, A. R., author.
Title: What is fake news? / by A. R. Carser.
Description: San Diego, CA: BrightPoint Press, [2023] | Series: Questions explored | Includes bibliographical references and index. | Audience: Grades 7-9
Identifiers: LCCN 2022029136 (print) | LCCN 2022029137 (eBook) | ISBN 9781678205089 (hardcover) | ISBN 9781678205096 (pdf)
Subjects: LCSH: Fake news--Juvenile literature.
Classification: LCC PN4784.F27 C37 2023 (print) | LCC PN4784.F27 (eBook) | DDC 070.4/3--dc23/eng/20220712
LC record available at https://lccn.loc.gov/2022029136
LC eBook record available at https://lccn.loc.gov/2022029137

CONTENTS

AT A GLANCE   4

INTRODUCTION   6
FRUSTRATED BY FAKE NEWS

CHAPTER ONE   12
WHAT IS FAKE NEWS?

CHAPTER TWO   30
HOW DOES FAKE NEWS AFFECT PEOPLE?

CHAPTER THREE   44
HOW DOES FAKE NEWS AFFECT SOCIETY?

CHAPTER FOUR   58
HOW CAN PEOPLE DEAL WITH FAKE NEWS?

Glossary   74
Source Notes   75
For Further Research   76
Index   78
Image Credits   79
About the Author   80

AT A GLANCE

- Fake news is false or misleading information designed to look like truthful news. It includes misinformation, disinformation, rumors, lies, and propaganda.

- Social media platforms, websites, radio, podcasts, and television are common places people see and hear fake news.

- People, companies, and governments use fake news to achieve certain goals. They may want to protect their reputations or gain public support.

- People tend to pay more attention to negative news stories. This is called negativity bias.

- Confirmation bias makes people more likely to believe information that confirms what they already believe. This can happen even if the information is false.

- Group bias occurs when people favor other people who have similar beliefs. This can cause one group to treat another group unfairly.

- Sometimes news outlets can be biased. Often, this bias is unintentional. But some news outlets are intentionally biased toward a particular group.

- People can reduce the influence of fake news. They can use reliable sources, understand how fake news spreads, and stay up to date on current events.

INTRODUCTION

FRUSTRATED BY FAKE NEWS

Maya had one week before her big report was due. It was the final project in her eighth-grade science class. She was stumped. Her report was about climate change. She needed to include five reliable sources. She searched for "climate change" on Instagram. Many accounts and posts appeared. But the results were

It can be hard to tell if information is true or false. This can make searching for online sources frustrating.

confusing. Some posts shared photos of wildfires and floods. They said climate change contributed to these events. Other posts claimed climate change was not real.

Maya was not sure what to believe. She searched "Is climate change real?" on Google. The first few results said yes. But then she found other sites that said the opposite. Frustrated, she closed her laptop. She would have to ask her teacher for help.

The next day, Maya spoke with her teacher, Ms. Allen. Ms. Allen said that finding out the truth can be difficult. Some people share false information online. Others bend the truth so it fits what they believe. Climate change is a controversial topic in the United States. Most people believe it is happening. But other people

Many people spread false information online, especially on social media.

deny it. Ms. Allen said that it was Maya's job to find sources that shared the truth.

Ms. Allen suggested looking up websites with ".gov" in their addresses. These are websites run by the US government. Most experts consider the US government a reliable source of information.

Making sure online sources are credible and trustworthy can help people feel more confident in their research.

It was almost time for Maya's next class. As Maya gathered her things, Ms. Allen shared one more idea. She told Maya to look for **consensus**. If nine out of ten sources agree, the information is most likely true.

That night, Maya typed "climate change .gov" into her search bar. Hundreds of US government websites appeared. Then she searched "climate change New York Times." Maya read through a dozen articles and websites. They all agreed that climate change was real. Maya smiled. She was on the right track.

CHAPTER ONE

WHAT IS FAKE NEWS?

Finding the truth is not easy. Most people think they can trust what they read online. They believe they can trust what they hear on the news. But this is not always the case. People, companies, and governments can be untruthful. This may be by accident or on purpose. When trusted sources are untruthful, it confuses people.

Encountering false information online or in the news can confuse people.

People struggle to know what is real and what is fake.

Fake news is false or misleading information designed to look like real news. It often happens when a person, company, or government is untruthful on

Sometimes people share fake news by accident, but others spread disinformation on purpose.

purpose. Some fake news is misinformation. Misinformation is incorrect or false information. A person who spreads misinformation may or may not realize he is being untruthful. Other fake news is disinformation. Disinformation is information that a person knows is false. But she shares it on social media, on TV, or in newspapers anyway.

Fake news can also include rumors and lies. A rumor is a statement with an unknown source. No one knows where the information came from. It is difficult to know if a rumor is true or false. Rumors often appear after an emergency. This occurs because facts are not always readily available or understandable. A lie is an untrue statement someone makes on purpose.

In extreme cases, fake news turns into propaganda. Propaganda is information used to support a particular political view or cause. Often, this information is misleading or false. It is used to change what people think about that view or cause. Propaganda is often used to grow public support for government policies.

Spotting fake news can be difficult. It often appears alongside real news or facts. Fake news is common on social media platforms. Brendan Nyhan is a professor of government studies at Dartmouth College. He explains how social media can spread fake news. "Facebook, Google, and Twitter function as . . . [platforms] for circulating false information and helping find receptive audiences," he says.[1] Social media makes it easy to share fake news. Users do not need to read or understand a post to share it.

CONSPIRACY THEORIES

A conspiracy theory is an idea that a secret, powerful organization is responsible for an event. One conspiracy theory is that the US government faked the moon landing. Conspiracy theories are not true. But more than half of Americans believe at least one conspiracy theory. People use them to explain confusing, emotional events. The theories offer a simple reason why the event happened. But that reason is often highly unlikely or impossible. Conspiracy theories are powerful. They give structure to chaotic events. They confirm what people want to believe.

Many people encounter fake news on social media platforms. These platforms make it easier for fake news to spread.

When a person shares fake news, more people end up seeing it. It may make them believe something that is not true. Or it may **reinforce** an existing belief that is untrue.

Fake news may also appear in other places. Websites can share fake news.

So can podcasts and radio shows. Fake news can be found on TV too.

WHY FAKE NEWS WORKS

Fake news tricks people into thinking it is real. It is designed to feel like real news. Kay Mathiesen is a professor of philosophy. She studies information and computer **ethics**. "Fake news gets traction by fooling people into thinking it has the . . . **legitimacy** of real news. In other words, it is made to look like or sound like legitimate news," Mathiesen explains.[2]

This makes fake news a powerful tool. People, companies, and governments use

Fake news is often designed to look and feel like real news.

fake news to achieve certain goals. For example, a person may use fake news to protect her reputation. A politician may lie about his actions or opinions to stay popular with supporters. Or a person may use fake news to destroy someone else's reputation. A company may use fake news to convince consumers its products are safe. A government may use fake news to grow public support for its policies.

FAKE NEWS IS NOT NEW

People, companies, and governments have used fake news throughout history. In the late 1850s, fake news was used to defend slavery in the United States. Southern newspapers made false claims about Abraham Lincoln. They claimed Lincoln's election would cause violence. They said enslaved people would revolt. The South would burn. These claims were intended to cause fear in white Southerners. They were

Even after Abraham Lincoln won the 1860 presidential election, proslavery newspapers claimed that he hated the South and would destroy its way of life.

meant to strengthen people's support of slavery.

In the 1890s, fake news was very common. Newspapers competed with each other for readers. They published shocking stories. Many stories stretched the truth. Others outright lied. In early 1898, a US battleship called the *Maine* sank in Havana, Cuba. Cuba was a Spanish colony. An accident caused the ship to sink.

FAKE PHOTOS IN HISTORY

Photos and videos can be fake news. President Ulysses S. Grant was a general in the US Civil War (1861–1865). A 1902 photo shows him on a Civil War battlefield. But the photo is fake. It was created by combining three different images. And during World War II (1939–1945), Soviet leaders often removed political enemies from photos. Soviet dictator Josef Stalin had many of his political enemies murdered. When he did, these people were often removed from photos.

In the 1890s, many newspapers published sensational, shocking stories. In 1898, newspapers spread false claims that the US battleship Maine was destroyed by the Spanish.

But two newspaper publishers claimed the Spanish were to blame. The US public believed the papers. Support for war with Spain grew. The Spanish-American War started later that year.

Another example of fake news came in the 1950s. In 1954, over 400 newspapers published a statement from the Tobacco Industry Research Committee (TIRC). At the time, scientists had discovered that smoking caused lung cancer. The TIRC claimed this was not true. It said scientists did not agree that smoking caused lung cancer. It claimed tobacco products were not harmful.

Tobacco companies ran the TIRC. They knew about the link between tobacco use and lung cancer. If people stopped smoking, the companies would lose money.

The companies formed the TIRC to cast doubt on the scientific findings. It was part of their strategy to keep customers.

Over the next three decades, tobacco companies also created false advertisements. These ads said people could not trust the science. They said more research was needed. In 1998, a court case revealed the industry's use of fake news and false ads.

Fake news gained attention during the 2016 presidential election. In 2016, one popular fake news story was a conspiracy theory. It became known as Pizzagate.

In the 1950s, tobacco companies were eager to avoid losing customers. Many tobacco ads at the time told people that cigarettes were not harmful.

People on social media spread a false claim about Democratic candidate Hillary Clinton and other Democrats. People claimed

During his campaigns and presidency, Donald Trump made thousands of false claims, including some that repeated information from fake news stories. Journalists and researchers fact-checked statements made by Trump and other politicians.

that these leaders were running a child trafficking ring at a pizza restaurant. The story spread quickly. Many people believed it was true. The story made them distrust

Clinton and other Democratic candidates. It even led to dangerous situations, such as a man bringing a gun to the pizza restaurant.

Meanwhile, Republican candidate Donald Trump accused news networks of publishing fake news. He claimed those sources treated him unfairly. This use of the term "fake news" **discredited** the networks with the public.

Fake news is a powerful tool. It affects individuals as well as society. But by learning how to spot fake news, people can stop it from spreading.

CHAPTER TWO

HOW DOES FAKE NEWS AFFECT PEOPLE?

People want to understand the world around them. They want to know why and how events happen. They want to learn how situations might affect them personally. It is natural for humans to be curious. In the past, thinking about these things kept people safe from dangers.

People want to understand why and how things happen. This need for understanding can lead them to believe rumors or misinformation.

In the modern era, this need can lead people to believe untrue claims. When an event occurs, rumors and misinformation spread. Facts may not be immediately available to learn. Other times, facts are complicated. People may not understand them. In these cases, people may choose to believe rumors and misinformation. False claims often simplify the details of an event. They provide an explanation that is easy to understand. This may be true even if the explanation is unlikely. People might believe these claims to make sense of the event.

Once a person learns a piece of information, unlearning it is difficult. When the brain hears something repeatedly, it remembers it. When information is heard over and over again, the brain has a hard time believing the information is false. This is the case with firmly held beliefs too. If a person passionately believes something, it is hard for him to reject it. This is true even if the belief is false. When people believe fake news, it can be hard for them to accept the truth.

COGNITIVE DISSONANCE

Cognitive dissonance happens when the facts do not match a person's views and beliefs. For example, a person might believe Earth is flat. Then he sees a photograph of the planet from space. Earth is clearly round. This new information does not match his beliefs. This is an uncomfortable feeling. People avoid the discomfort of cognitive dissonance. They may ignore the facts. Or they may come up with an explanation to discredit the facts.

Negativity bias can make a person more likely to focus on negative news stories.

BIAS AND FAKE NEWS

The way the brain processes and remembers information creates bias. Bias is a personal judgment. People make judgments about the information they learn.

One type of bias is negativity bias. The brain is wired to focus on possible dangers. In modern times, this makes humans focus on negative news. If the news is negative, people pay attention. They are more likely to remember it. This is true of negative fake news too. These stories may be memorable, even if the information is false.

People are also more likely to believe information that confirms something they already believe. This is called confirmation bias. For example, fans of a football team may believe their team is always in the right. This cannot always be true. But fans' confirmation bias makes them believe it is. Fake news articles may be untrue. But they may confirm a reader's views. Confirmation bias causes the reader to believe the articles.

Negativity bias and confirmation bias affect how people process news. Michael Lynch is a professor of philosophy. He studies fake news. "Fake news has the effect of getting people not to believe real things," he explains. Lynch says fake news can make people doubt that truth exists. This makes them ignore facts. "There's no way for [people] to know what is objectively

People are more likely to believe information that confirms what they already believe.

true. . . . [They will] ignore the facts because nobody knows what's really true anyway."[3] People who create fake news know this. They create stories that play to people's biases.

Social media has changed the way people get news. Most young adults get their news on social media platforms.

SOCIAL MEDIA AND THE NEWS

A 2020 survey found that about 86 percent of US adults get their news online. They use smartphones, computers, or tablets. Many of these people read news websites or use news apps. But a growing number of people get their news on social media. This is especially true of young adults. This group is most likely to use social media to get their news.

> **FACTS VERSUS OPINIONS**
>
> A fact is something that can be proven. "The United States is a country" is a fact. An opinion is a belief, thought, or feeling. "The United States is the greatest country in the world" is an opinion. Trustworthy news sources rely on facts. They share dates, locations, and numbers to prove a claim is true. People cannot disagree with facts. Opinion articles share the thoughts and beliefs of a person or group. It is possible for a person to disagree with an opinion. Some reliable news sources also run opinion articles. Readers should note whether an article is a news piece or an opinion piece.

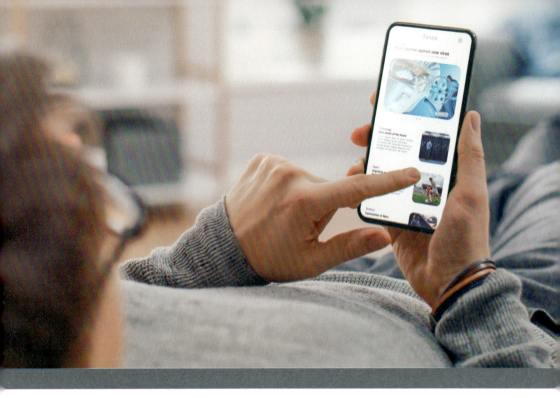

Social media algorithms fill users' feeds with content similar to posts they have viewed or liked before.

People who use social media are more likely to see fake news. They are also more likely to believe it. People share social media posts with misinformation. This means false information can show up repeatedly in a user's feed. The brain is more likely to remember the false information as true.

Confirmation and negativity bias also play roles on social media. Social media users are more likely to share information that confirms what they believe. They are more likely to share information that is negative too. This spreads fake news.

When a user reacts to and shares fake news, she sees more of it. Social media platforms use computer programs called **algorithms**. Algorithms decide what people see in their news feeds. The algorithms want news feeds to be engaging.

They want to make sure people keep using the app. They show content similar to what users viewed and shared before. Jim VandeHei is the CEO of news organization Axios. He warns users about these algorithms. "Remember: If your Facebook feed is filled with garbage, it means you were reading garbage in the first place," he says. "The algorithm simply gives you more of what you crave."[4]

Fake news can make people distrust what they see and hear. It misleads people into believing things that are untrue. This causes people to distrust any news source,

People can fight against fake news by learning how to spot it.

even if it is truthful. This is what gives fake news its power. It is why it is important to be able to spot fake news.

CHAPTER THREE

HOW DOES FAKE NEWS AFFECT SOCIETY?

In November 2016, Donald Trump won the US presidential election. During his campaign, Trump sometimes spread false information. He criticized the journalists, newspapers, and TV networks that corrected his claims. At the same time, fake news articles appeared online. In October

During Trump's presidential campaign, he tried to sway public opinion by accusing reputable news networks of publishing fake news.

2016, 6.6 million posts on Twitter featured fake news articles. These articles were published by websites that wrote misleading or false content. Millions of voters saw and shared these articles. Trump himself sometimes repeated claims made in fake news articles.

The Pew Foundation conducted a survey of US voters in December 2016. It found that Trump's claims and online fake news had influenced public opinion. Two-thirds of the people surveyed said fake news stories were confusing. The stories made it hard to understand current events and issues. A third of the people surveyed said they had seen fake news online. A quarter admitted to sharing news they knew was fake.

THE 2020 PRESIDENTIAL ELECTION

Trump continued to spread false information before the 2020 presidential election. He and his campaign said that if 2020

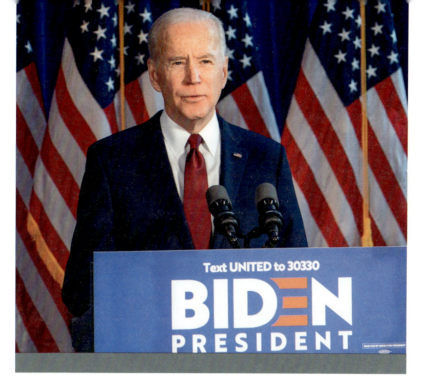

During the 2020 presidential campaign, many people read and shared fake news stories. Some of them spread false information about Democratic candidate Joe Biden.

challenger Joe Biden won the election, the election was stolen. Trump made false claims of election **fraud**. He claimed Biden was corrupt. Many Trump supporters believed this claim. Meanwhile, fake news stories about mail-in voting spread.

Trump's false claims about election fraud encouraged his supporters to attack the US Capitol on January 6, 2021.

People claimed mail-in ballots were being thrown away. This increased some people's distrust of the election process.

Biden won the 2020 election. Groups of Trump supporters organized on social media. They called their movement Stop the Steal. They were influenced by fake news stories that backed up Trump's claims about election fraud. Some of these groups wanted to use violence to prevent Biden from becoming president. They went to Washington, DC, on

> **CLICKBAIT**
>
> Fake news spreads quickly. Many fake news articles and headlines are written to grab attention. This type of content is called clickbait. Clickbait headlines get people to click on links. "Pope Francis Shocks World, Endorses Donald Trump for President" is a clickbait headline from July 2016. It was not true. But nearly 1 million people liked, shared, or clicked on it.

January 6, 2021. This was when Congress certified the presidential election results. Trump supporters attended a rally near the US Capitol. Trump encouraged the crowd to take action. His supporters marched to the Capitol and violently attacked it.

Trump was not the first powerful person to use fake news. Politicians, political groups, and businesses use fake news too. It is easy to spread misinformation. People and companies can publish books and pamphlets. They can appear on TV or radio. They can create websites and social media accounts. People can pay for ads

Fake news can be shared through TV, ads, magazines, radio shows, books, and more.

in newspapers, on TV, and online. They can make these ads look like news stories. People might not realize they are looking at a paid ad. The public sees these messages frequently and repeatedly. Even if the messages are misleading, people can start to believe them.

GROUP BIAS

Confirmation bias and negativity bias affect what individuals believe. These biases influence the news they see online, whether it is fake or real. But bias can affect groups too.

One study showed bias among political groups. The 2020 study was completed by researchers at the University of Cambridge and Northeastern University. Conservative people tended to believe left-leaning news outlets were fake news. People who were liberal tended to believe right-leaning news outlets were fake news. But "the fake news effect appears more pronounced among conservative audiences," researchers said.[5]

Group bias can have consequences. People tend to favor others with similar beliefs. This can cause members of one

SCHOLARLY VERSUS POPULAR SOURCES

When researching a subject for a school project, it is hard to know when to trust a source. This is especially true when online search results mix scholarly sources with popular ones. Scholarly sources are written by professors, researchers, and other experts. They are published in academic journals and reviewed by other experts. Popular sources can be written by anyone. They may appear in magazines or blogs. Some popular sources are well-researched and accurate. Others are not.

Some news sources may have a conservative or liberal bias. They are written for an audience that shares this bias.

group to treat another group unfairly. Sometimes, group bias leads people to act dishonestly or immorally.

Bias affects journalists too. Some journalists unintentionally allow their biases to influence news coverage. They may stick to the facts within a story. But their biases may cause them to decide one story is more important than another. For example, an urban news outlet may ignore stories about rural areas.

Bias in the news can also be intentional. Some magazines are meant for particular audiences. The *National Review* is a conservative magazine written for conservatives. The *Nation* is a liberal magazine meant for liberals. Articles in these magazines may be accurate. But they are written to appeal to their intended audiences. Articles may emphasize some facts while ignoring others. Readers may not get the complete story.

SPREADING DISTRUST

Fake news builds distrust in news sources and the government. In the United States, the public has political power through voting. People need accurate information to make informed choices. Fake news makes it hard for the public to separate fact from fiction.

People need to believe leaders are trustworthy sources of information. Scott McClellan was President George W. Bush's press secretary. He warned that

Fake news can make people distrust news sources and the government, which may impact how they vote.

lying and embracing fake news can harm democracy. In a 2022 interview, he spoke about the Trump administration. He said, "You're speaking for the free world to some extent. . . . What ideals are you holding up for that free world?"[6]

CHAPTER FOUR

HOW CAN PEOPLE DEAL WITH FAKE NEWS?

Fake news is almost impossible to avoid. Misinformation and disinformation are spread on TV, radio, and the internet. False claims can be found in newspapers, on podcasts, and on social media. Even billboards may be

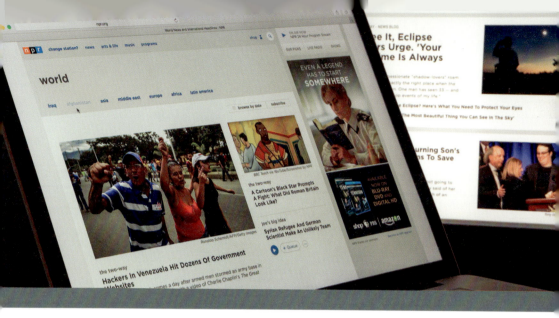

Getting news from reliable and unbiased sources is a good way to avoid fake news and reduce its influence.

used to spread fake news. Fake news is everywhere. So people must be able to spot it. They need to know how to **debunk** it.

Fake news might be everywhere. But people can reduce its influence. First, they can get their news from reliable sources. Newspaper articles are often reliable sources. So are network TV news programs and websites run by the US government. Reliable sources agree on the facts. They **fact-check** their articles to make sure they are true. They may also fact-check

> ### FACT-CHECKING THE NEWS
>
> Reliable news sources fact-check the information they share with the public. They want to provide accurate, unbiased information. Other fact checkers review information that public figures share. They check the accuracy of popular social media posts. The Associated Press, Reuters, and the *Washington Post* publish fact-checking webpages. People can visit them to learn if a story is fake. The websites Snopes and PolitiFact review statements and online posts. They rate how accurate or misleading different claims are.

Journalists who work for reliable news sources fact-check claims, stories, and other information to make sure they are accurate.

statements that public figures make. This includes politicians, business leaders, and others.

Next, people can understand how fake news spreads. They can learn how social media algorithms work. Users can be careful about the social media pages they follow. They can think twice before liking or sharing a post. Just a few sources create most fake news content. Other sites share and spread this content. When people stop sharing fake news, its power fades.

Finally, people can keep up with current events. They can get their news from reliable sources. This way, people can learn the truth about the issues they care about. When they see fake news, they will know it is untrue.

STOP AND THINK

Knowing which sources to trust is not easy. Researching sources takes time. It requires critical thinking skills. These skills do not

Critical thinking skills can help people accurately interpret information. These skills can help them figure out if information is trustworthy.

teach a person what to believe. They teach people how to know if a source is reliable. Critical thinking involves asking questions about the information in a source.

People should not believe everything they read or see. They should question the accuracy of what they learn. One tip is

Teachers and librarians can help teens find reliable sources.

to check the age of the information. Is the story current? Or is it a few years old? Events and stories can change over time. New information can be added.

People should also research a story's author. Is the author who he claims to be?

Is he a journalist or an expert on the topic? Is he a politician? If so, what are his political beliefs? How might these beliefs affect how the author presents the facts?

A person should reflect on her own beliefs and biases too. Do her beliefs make it easier or more difficult to believe a story? Does she know the author's beliefs? Do those beliefs align with her own beliefs?

Developing critical thinking skills takes practice. Teachers and librarians can help students practice these skills. They can point students toward reliable sources. They can also help students become more

TIPS FOR EVALUATING SOURCES

Look for a recent publication date.

Research the author to confirm he or she is reliable and credible.

Research the website to confirm it is reliable and credible.

Consider if the information is based on facts.

Check other reliable sources to confirm the claims.

Look for citations and quotes from experts.

Be skeptical of sources with lots of advertising.

Ask a teacher or librarian for help.

Source: Cindy L. Otis, *True or False: A CIA Analyst's Guide to Spotting Fake News. New York: Feiwel and Friends, 2020.* pp. 208-14.

Evaluating sources takes practice. Here are a few tips for finding out whether or not a source is fake news.

aware of their own biases. Dr. Jimmeka Guillory Wright is a psychologist. She says, "Hopefully by increasing awareness we can start to help our students become more aware of their own bias and help them to be able to identify misinformation when they encounter it."[7]

FAKE NEWS AND THE LAW

Fake news can cause harm to individuals and society. People may wonder why it is allowed to be published. The First Amendment of the US Constitution guarantees the right to free speech. People and organizations have the right to publish

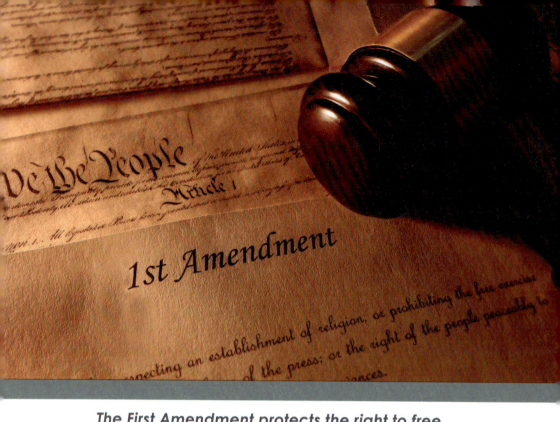

The First Amendment protects the right to free speech. This means that people have the right to share information, even if it is false.

and share information. The Supreme Court has ruled that this includes offensive or false information. The Supreme Court has also ruled that speech cannot be restricted if it does not cause harm. This is true even when that speech is false.

Section 230 of the Communications Decency Act of 1996 protects online companies. This includes websites and social media platforms. Companies are not

IS FACEBOOK TO BLAME?

Facebook allowed disinformation to spread in the 2016 and 2020 presidential elections. In 2016, Russian accounts bought ads on Facebook. They posted and shared misleading or false content. More than 126 million users saw Russian-generated content. In 2020, Facebook allowed political ads with misleading information. This caused lies to spread. In 2021, a former Facebook employee testified before Congress. She claimed Facebook was causing harm by allowing fake news to spread. But Facebook claimed this was not true. It said that it had worked to stop misleading political ads.

responsible for information that users share on their platforms. They may choose to take down user content. Or they may choose to leave it up. However, Section 230 also says that online platforms will be held responsible if they support or share content that goes against federal law.

THE FUTURE OF FAKE NEWS

Fake news has been around for a long time. Experts believe it will continue into the future. Dr. Nicole A. Cooke is a professor of communication, information, and library studies. She explains that fake news might be called another name someday. But it

New technology, including phone cameras that can scan people's faces, has made it easier for everyday people to create realistic fake images.

will still be around. "When the fake news moniker has faded, the problem will still exist, and eventually reemerge with a new name," she says.[8]

Fake news is already evolving. Deepfake images and videos are now possible. Deepfakes are images and videos that have

Metaliteracy can help students develop skills for navigating social media. It teaches them how to spot fake news and find reliable sources.

been digitally altered. People usually trust that images and videos are real. It used to be difficult to create a fake image or video. But new technologies make it easy. People should evaluate images and videos for accuracy. For example, they can search for the image or video online. Often, deepfakes can be debunked by finding the original image or video.

Checking for deepfakes is one part of metaliteracy. This is a new field of critical thinking. It applies critical thinking skills to social media and other online sources. Students may learn metaliteracy skills in school. This helps them adapt their critical thinking skills to new types of media. Metaliteracy may become an important way to deal with fake news. It will be a tool people can use to spot fake news and uncover the truth.

GLOSSARY

algorithms

step-by-step processes for producing search results online

consensus

general agreement among a group of people or sources

debunk

to expose as false

discredited

caused someone to disbelieve a claim, or refused to accept something as true

ethics

a set of moral values

fact-check

to investigate and verify whether information is true

fraud

intentional deception or trickery

legitimacy

being a genuine, actual example of something

reinforce

to strengthen an idea with additional evidence

SOURCE NOTES

CHAPTER ONE: WHAT IS FAKE NEWS?

1. Quoted in Benedict Carey, "How Fiction Becomes Fact on Social Media," *New York Times*, October 20, 2017. www.nytimes.com.

2. Kay Mathiesen, "Fighting Fake News," *Information Literacy and Libraries in the Age of Fake News*. Edited by Denise E. Agosto, Santa Barbara, CA: Libraries Unlimited, 2018. p. 79.

CHAPTER TWO: HOW DOES FAKE NEWS AFFECT PEOPLE?

3. Quoted in Sabrina Tavernise, "As Fake News Spreads Lies, More Readers Shrug at the Truth," *New York Times*, December 6, 2016. www.nytimes.com.

4. Quoted in James W. Cortada and William Aspray, *Fake News Nation.* Lanham, MD: Rowman & Littlefield, 2019. p. vii.

CHAPTER THREE: HOW DOES FAKE NEWS AFFECT SOCIETY?

5. Quoted in Sander van der Linden, et al., "You Are Fake News," *Media, Culture & Society*, vol. 42, no. 3, April 2020, pp. 460–470.

6. Quoted in Jim Rutenberg, "'Alternative Facts' and the Costs of Trump-Branded Reality," *New York Times*, January 22, 2017. www.nytimes.com.

CHAPTER FOUR: HOW CAN PEOPLE DEAL WITH FAKE NEWS?

7. Quoted in Stephanie Pappas, "Fighting Fake News in the Classroom," *American Psychological Association*, January 1, 2022. www.apa.org.

8. Quoted in Cortada and Aspray, *Fake News Nation*, p. 211.

FOR FURTHER RESEARCH

BOOKS

Robin Terry Brown, *Breaking the News: What's Real, What's Not, and Why the Difference Matters*. Washington, DC: National Geographic Kids, 2020.

Kari A. Cornell, *Fake News*. San Diego, CA: BrightPoint Press, 2020.

Dona Herweck Rice, *Deception: Real or Fake News?* Huntington Beach, CA: Teacher Created Materials, 2018.

INTERNET SOURCES

"Fake News: How to Spot It," *Maryland State Library Resource Center*, n.d. www.slrc.info.

"Trump's False or Misleading Claims Total 30,573 Over 4 Years," *Washington Post*, January 20, 2021. www.washingtonpost.com.

Darrell M. West, "How to Combat Fake News and Disinformation," *Brookings Institution*, December 18, 2017. www.brookings.edu.

WEBSITES

AP Fact Check
https://apnews.com/hub/ap-fact-check

The AP Fact Check blog debunks popular fake news articles.

Doubt It or Trust It?
https://doubtit.ca

The Doubt It or Trust It? site provides fact-checking resources, tips about how to spot fake news, and fun quizzes.

News and Media Literacy Collection
https://tpt.pbslearningmedia.org/collection/newsandmedialiteracy/t/fake-news/

The News and Media Literacy Collection provides activities and videos about learning how to spot fake news and misinformation online.

INDEX

advertising, 26, 50–51, 66, 69
algorithms, 41–42, 61

bias, 34–37, 41, 52–55, 65, 67
    confirmation bias, 35–36, 41, 52
    group bias, 52–54
    negativity bias, 35, 36, 41, 52
Biden, Joe, 47–49

clickbait, 49
Clinton, Hillary, 27–29
cognitive dissonance, 33
Communications Decency Act of 1996, 69–70
consensus, 11
conspiracy theories, 17, 26–29
Cooke, Nicole A., 70–71
critical thinking skills, 62–65, 66, 73

deepfakes, 71–73
disinformation, 14–15, 58, 69

evaluating sources, 62–65, 66, 67, 72–73

Facebook, 16–17, 42, 69
fact-checking, 60–61
First Amendment, 67–69
fraud, 47–49

journalists, 44, 54–55, 60–61, 65

Lincoln, Abraham, 21–22
Lynch, Michael, 36–37

Maine, 23–24
Mathiesen, Kay, 19
McClellan, Scott, 56–57
metaliteracy, 73
misinformation, 14, 31–32, 40, 50, 58, 67

Nyhan, Brendan, 16–17

Pizzagate, 26–29
popular sources, 53
propaganda, 15–16

reliable sources, 6, 9, 39, 53, 59–61, 62–67
rumors, 15, 31–32

scholarly sources, 53
social media, 15, 16–18, 27, 38–42, 45, 48–49, 50, 58, 60, 61–62, 69–70, 73
Spanish-American War, 23–24
Stop the Steal, 48–50

Tobacco Industry Research Committee (TIRC), 25–26
Trump, Donald, 29, 44–50, 57
Twitter, 16–17, 45

VandeHei, Jim, 42
voting, 47–48, 56

Wright, Jimmeka Guillory, 67

IMAGE CREDITS

Cover: © Africa Studio/Shutterstock Images
5: © Moore Media/iStockphoto
7: © Xavier Lorenzo/iStockphoto
9: © Primakov/Shutterstock Images
10: © Ground Picture/Shutterstock Images
13: © Deepak Sethi/iStockphoto
14: © Gorodenkoff/Shutterstock Images
18: © Raw Pixel/Shutterstock Images
20: © Oatawa/iStockphoto
22: © Everett Collection/Shutterstock Images
24: © Everett Collection/Shutterstock Images
27: © Wwing/iStockphoto
28: © Ascannio/Shutterstock Images
31: © Grinvalds/iStockphoto
34: © Valeriy G./iStockphoto
37: © Prostock Studio/iStockphoto
38: © Twin Design/Shutterstock Images
40: © Gorodenkoff/Shutterstock Images
43: © Capuski/iStockphoto
45: © Evan El-Amin/Shutterstock Images
47: © Lev Radin/Shutterstock Images
48: © Lev Radin/Shutterstock Images
51: © Copyright Lawrey/Shutterstock Images
54: © Hadrian/Shutterstock Images
57: © Rob Crandall/Shutterstock Images
59: © Casimiro PT/Shutterstock Images
61: © Alexander Khitrov/Shutterstock Images
63: © Kateryna Onyshchuk/iStockphoto
64: © Andres R./iStockphoto
66 (top row; second row; right): © Four Leaf Lover/Shutterstock Images
66 (second row; left; fourth row; right): © Davooda/Shutterstock Images
66 (third row): © Davooda/Shutterstock Images
66 (fourth row; left): © Ksenvitaln/Shutterstock Images
68: © Zimmytws/Shutterstock Images
71: © Tzido/iStockphoto
72: © Drazen Zigic/iStockphoto

ABOUT THE AUTHOR

A. R. Carser is a freelance writer who lives in Minnesota. She enjoys learning and writing about history, politics, and media.